DAILY RECORD

50p

10/-

CONTENTS

FOOTBALL . . . it's a magic word in Scotland. It means excitement, drama, tears, and happiness to thousands of fans. In this book the 'Daily Record' brings you the inside stories of the world of football. Stories told by some of the biggest names in the game. Names such as Willie Waddell, Neil Mochan, Pat Stanton and Bobby Calder.

Scotland's top sports writers are also here; the men who have travelled the world on the big football stories. Hugh Taylor, Alex Cameron, Ken Gallacher, the men who know the players, managers, scouts even the groundsmen in football-crazy Scotland.

In picture form we bring you all the excitement of the colourful world of soccer, frozen in action by expert photographers. It's all inside. Come in and join us.

**Jack Adams
Sports Editor
'Daily Record'**

WE IN SCOTLAND like to think we invented football. Alas, we didn't. It is true, however, that this little country of ours did more for the game that is now the world's most popular than anyone else. For it was Scotland who really taught the world to play football.

Scotland, of course, has been playing football of one kind or another for many centuries and an old poem, dating probably from the 15th century, reads:

"Dislocated muscles and broken bones,
Strife, discord and ruined homes,
Twisted in old age, then crippled as well–
These are the beauties of the football!"

No one really knows how the game was played in those far-off days; but you can bet it was a rough pastime with probably one half of a town facing the other. The rules? Anything went, from mayhem to medieval mocking of the referee, if there was one!

England, however, takes credit for organising the game in the last century, though it was not long before Scottish footballers were eagerly sought by English clubs because of the superior style and technique developed north of the border.

High tribute was paid to the Scots when Vale of Leven travelled to London in 1878 to beat the renowned Wanderers at Kennington Oval in a mighty clash between lusty heroes in whiskers, long pants, shinguards worn outside stockings and clumsy boots.

Long before this in the 1820s a big battle raged between two main schools of thought as to how football should be played – "hands" or "no hands". The "Cambridge Rules" were drawn up in 1848 for football enthusiasts by old boys of Eton, Harrow, Winchester, Rugby and Shrewsbury, but these were primitive and the game continued to vary its laws up and down the country.

Clubs had sprung up in Sheffield by the time the English Football Association held their first meeting in

The Game Scotland Taught the World

London, to be followed by the publication of the first rules on December 1, 1863. Four years later, in 1867, Queen's Park was formed and Association Football came to Scotland.

From the early 1870s it was Queen's Park who led the way in football and Queen's Park who set the style. Their record in Scotland was almost incredible.

In July, 1867, they played so brilliantly that they did not concede a single goal until January, 1875 – and that was to Vale of Leven. It was a national calamity when, on February 5, 1876, Queen's was defeated for the first time, by the Wanderers in London.

Queen's Park looked on the Scottish Cup as its own personal property. From the time the competition began in the season 1873-74, Queen's won it each year until season 1876-77 and without losing a goal.

Indeed, the story of Scottish football in the early days is the story of Queen's Park. And Queen's did more than anyone else to make the game international.

In 1872, Queen's had reached a top standard in football and it applied for admission to the only governing body in existence, the F.A. of England.

Queen's became famous over the border, as well. In 1872, they drew with the mighty Wanderers in an English Cup-tie and assumed the great responsibility of playing the first international match against England, providing all the Scottish players and holding their opponents to a 0–0 draw.

The success of one club against a nation in this international gave an astonishing impetus to football in Scotland, and the number of clubs increased rapidly. No longer was Queen's Park in splendid isolation for they began to find plenty of opposition at home, with rivals including Kilmarnock, Dumbarton, Vale of Leven and Rangers, all formed during 1872-73.

by Hugh Taylor

QUEEN'S PARK FOOTBALL CLUB

Here they are, the first Scottish Cup Winners, the great Queen's Park team of 1873-74. For the soccer historian the team reads: Back row: A. McKinnon, J. Dixon, T. Lawrie, C. Campbell, R. W. Neil. Front row: R. Leckie, J. Taylor, H. McNeil, J. J. Thomson, J. B. Weir, W. McKinnon.

Football was growing up and still Queen's Park was the source of every new move. They found great players. They evolved new tactics. And they had officials in every new organisation.

Queen's worked for progress, developed style of play, swept away anomalies and introduced new rules.

For instance, the rules on which Queen's Park had to work in the late 1860s were those of the English Association and the Rugby influence was apparent in terms such as "a fair catch", "touch down" and "modified handling". It took time, but Queen's was instrumental in modernising the rules. Here's an example: in 1875 Queen's suggested these amendments to the laws:

1 – To authorise the use of a goal bar, instead of a tape.
2 – To adopt a fixed half-time in playing, irrespective of goals being scored.
3 – To adopt a more explicit rule regarding the law of free kicks.

As far as tactics were concerned, Queen's Park turned football into a scientific game, making full use of teamwork, using, indeed, plans that seem new today.

Let's recall that first international. Hero of the day was a Queen's Park full-back, W. Kerr, of whom it was reported: "one run of his, from his base to the enemy's goal, electrified the crowd".

So, what's new? We like to think that attacking runs by Tommy Gemmell or John Greig are novel. But in those early days Queen's put the accent on attack, their line-up being a goalkeeper, two backs, two half-backs and six forwards.

England were even more attack-minded, fielding one 'keeper, one back, one half-back and eight forwards. They were so impressed by the Scottish style, though, that they adopted the Scottish formation for the next international and won 4–2!

In the early 1880s Scots were infiltrating into England's north, where professional teams were stealing all the thunder.

What did the early Scots earn as professionals? Well, Sunderland's "Team of all the Talents" who included the immortals, Doig, Gow, Wilson, Campbell, Auld and Miller, were paid a £10 bonus on engagement and received weekly wages of 25s. Then the wages were increased to the fabulous sum of £3 a week, all the year round – big money in the 90s!

Meanwhile, back home in

It may still look old-fashioned, but to the old-timers at Queen's Park this 1902 Hearts team group would look very modern. Some of the moustaches are still there but the shorts no longer meet the stockings and the boots now have studs, and what if one player still wears his shinguards outside his socks, old habits die hard.

Scotland, Queen's Park was still supreme, winning the Scottish Cup nine times between 1874 and 1893. But gradually others were taking the lead and professionalism was creeping in. Power was going into the hands of the S.F.A. and the Scottish League – and Queen's was taking a back seat.

The S.F.A. was formed in March, 1873, with the first clubs being Clydesdale, Dumbreck, Granville, Queen's Park, Rovers, Third Lanark and Vale of Leven.

The Scottish League was formed in Glasgow in 1890, with much opposition from Queen's Park, who feared the new body would favour professionalism – which turned out to be the case. The following clubs formed the new League: Rangers, Celtic, Dumbarton, Cambuslang, Third Lanark, Hearts, St. Mirren, Abercorn, Vale of Leven, Cowlairs and Renton.

Queen's battled on in opposition, playing clubs such as Thistle, Kilmarnock, Battlefield, St. Bernards, Hamilton Acas, Leith Athletic, Falkirk, Airdrieonians and various English clubs.

But most of these clubs joined the Scottish Alliance, soon to be the Scottish Second Division.

The writing was on the wall for Queen's. They had to join the League in 1900-01.

They were never again Scottish football history incarnate. But to Queen's the world owes a great debt. For it was the great Queen's Park who put Scottish football on the map.

And Scotland had taught the whole world a great, great game.

So YOU THINK you know all about football? Take the rules of the game . . . You know all about them of course. Or do you?

Well, here's a quiz, compiled by one of Scotland's top referees, that will test your knowledge – and, perhaps, help you win a few soccer arguments in the future.

1) A <u>direct</u> free kick is awarded to team 'A' just outside their penalty area, the centre-half quickly passes the ball back to his 'keeper but he is not ready for it, and the ball goes straight into the goal – what is your decision?

2) Why is there an arc of a circle drawn outside the penalty area?

3) What is decided by the toss of a coin at the beginning of the game?

4) Having added all the time for stoppages, there is only one occasion when time will be added. What is this occasion?

5) If the ball struck the corner flag post and rebounded into play the referee would let play continue. What would you do if it rebounded from the centre flag post?

6) Is the scissors kick legal?

7) Is standing in front of a goalkeeper at a corner kick obstruction?

8) A seasonal one. The centre-forward is running in on goal with only the 'keeper to beat, there is snow on the ground and the 'keeper is just inside the area. Quickly the goalkeeper gathers some snow and throws it at the centre-forward who is outside the area. What is your decision?

9) Give your decisions, and you have no time to stop and think about these,

9a) The centre plays the ball twice at a kick-off.

9b) The ball enters the goal direct from a corner kick.

9c) The ball enters the goal direct from a free kick for tripping.

9d) The ball enters the goal direct from a free kick for pushing.

9e) The ball enters the goal direct from a free kick for obstruction.

9f) The ball enters the goal direct from a free kick for dangerous play.

10) Finally – watch this one. An indirect free kick is awarded just outside the area, the players line up along the goal line and the kicker shoots hard for goal, the ball strikes one of his team mates standing on the goal line and passes on into the goal. What is your decision?

1) A corner kick, because Law 13 states a goal can be scored against the offending side only.

2) All players, except the goal-keeper and the player taking the kick, must be outside the penalty area and at least ten yards from the arc to the penalty mark. The arc to the spot is 10 yards and shows the referee that everyone behind this line must be far enough from the spot to allow the kick to be taken.

3) The winning captain can have either the choice of ends or the kick-off, and it has been known in the Scottish First Division games for the captain to choose the kick-off.

4) If a penalty kick has been awarded the referee will extend the time to permit the penalty kick to be taken.

5) Award a throw-in against the team whose player last played the ball, as the centre flag post is not on the line but at least one yard outside.

6) Yes. Provided there is no opposing player in the immediate vicinity of the kicker, then it would become dangerous play and an indirect free kick would be awarded.

7) If the player, when the ball is kicked, tries to play the ball normally then no offence has been committed. If, however, he jumps about to stop the goal-keeper from reaching the ball, then an indirect free kick would be awarded.

8) Having dealt with the 'keeper, you would award a penalty kick even though the centre-forward was struck outside the penalty area with the snowball. The place where the offence initiated is the key.

9a) A free kick for double play.
9b) A goal.
9c) A goal.
9d) A goal.
9e) A goal kick.
9f) A goal kick.

10) I told you to watch it. The answer must be off-side because if he was standing on the goal line he could not have had two opponents nearer the line than himself when the kick was taken.

THE "OLD FIRM" of Celtic and Rangers today stands commandingly over the rest of the Scottish clubs just as they have done since the Scottish League began some 80 years ago.

It is pointed out as a weakness in our national structure by English managers, players and supporters. It is criticised time and again by some of our own officials, players and supporters.

Yet it remains with us today as I feel it will always remain with us. And, I do not totally agree with those who say how bad it is for our football. I would like to see provincial teams getting more support from the "Old Firm" fans who leave Dunfermline and Kilmarnock, Dundee and Edinburgh, Aberdeen and Greenock, week after week to watch the Big Two.

But I believe that these teams must change their ways. It is no use sitting down in board rooms and complaining. It is no use looking back at the days after the war when football attendances soared to unheard-of proportions. These days have gone, and the clubs who refuse to spend the money they once drew in on ground improvements for the supporters are suffering for their lack of vision.

This will never happen to the "Old Firm". They are a way of life to so many people across Scotland. Even across the world.

I have been to the United States and Canada with both teams and have seen the fans there.

I have watched a broad main street in Toronto look like London Road, as buses emptied their green and white covered groups of supporters before a challenge game against Spurs.

I have met Rangers sup-

The tension's over and the "Old Firm" players can get back to being friends again after 90 minutes of the toughest football in the world.

The "Old Firm"

porters who have travelled from San Francisco to New York – 3,000 miles – simply to see their team play against, and beat, the Italian champions Fiorentina.

This is the strength of their loyalties, loyalties that have made them all-powerful. For those fans who would argue against the dominance of the Big Two it needs only for the record books to be brought out. Between them the "Old Firm" have always been top dogs. In the League

Championship, for instance, no team other than Celtic or Rangers won the title from 1905 until 1932, when Motherwell broke the stranglehold. The power of the "Old Firm" is not new!

There has been more variety in the Scottish Cup, but still no one can match the respective records of the deadly Glasgow rivals. For example in the last decade only one team, Dunfermline, who won the trophy twice, has broken through. Rangers

by Ken Gallacher

10

Dundee, Orjan Persson from Dundee United, and Colin Stein from Hibs.

The clubs who try to maintain a consistent challenge betray themselves by these sales. All of them help to strengthen the respective positions of the two giants at Parkhead and Ibrox.

In these days of substitutes and when player pools have become so necessary, no team in Scotland can match the reserve power of either Celtic or Rangers.

The one happy thought is that we do have two powerful teams in our relatively small country; two teams who are respected right across the continent of Europe; two teams who can match the best teams in England for financial and playing resources.

This is the consolation I cling to as I look at the economics of the game in Scotland. This, plus the fact that these are two teams that can reject any transfer move for their stars.

Celtic could have sold Jimmy Johnstone several times to England for record breaking fees, but the tiny redhead with the very special wing magic stays to delight his own countrymen.

Similarly, Rangers could have sat back and allowed

won it five times and Celtic three times.

Every year we look for a provincial challenge and every year that challenge begins bravely and then fades sadly away.

The clubs can complain as often as they like but it is a fact that Celtic has brought players from other Scottish sides – centre-forward Joe McBride from Motherwell, inside-forward Willie Wallace from Hearts, wing-half Tommy Callaghan from Dunfermline, goalkeeper Ronnie Simpson from Hibs, inside-forward Harry Hood from Clyde.

Rangers has been an even greater spender, buying Kai Johansen from Morton, Dave Smith from Aberdeen, Alex MacDonald from St. Johnstone, Andy Penman from

A moment of danger for Rangers as goalkeeper Gerry Neef punches a ball clear from the head of Celtic outside-left John Hughes and his own right-half John Greig.

Hibs to sell Colin Stein to Everton. Instead, they moved in, paid the first £100,000 fee in Scottish football history (it still remains the only one) and kept this personality goal-scorer north of the border.

The "Old Firm" helps to keep Scotland known and feared as a football nation.

But none of the facts I have so far stressed allow you to capture the great drawing power of the "Old Firm".

It is a League game which twice a season hoists the best attendance figures for League games in Britain, more than 70,000 seeing the game at Celtic Park and 80,000 watching at Ibrox. In their last meeting in the Scottish Cup Final at Hampden, there were 132,000 fans packing Europe's biggest ground. In one recent Glasgow Cup game, more than 90,000 fans swarmed into Ibrox to see a game that was little more than a friendly – if such a thing exists between these two soccer giants.

Sometimes the games live up to these fantastic crowds. Sometimes the tension proves too much for the players and the game falls short of its potential.

I know so many of the players who don't like the atmosphere of tension and strain that surrounds every meeting between the Glasgow greats. Yet none of these factors can affect the magic and the majesty of these occasions.

When you remember that so often Scottish soccer's major prizes are settled on the outcome of these games, then it is hard to disagree.

You can love them or you can loathe them, but you can never ignore the "Old Firm". Celtic and Rangers. Rangers and Celtic. One or other will be on the top – with their rivals hard on their heels – as long as Scottish soccer lives on.

Rangers' £100,000 centre Colin Stein finds out just how hard it is to beat Celtic centre-half Billy McNeill.

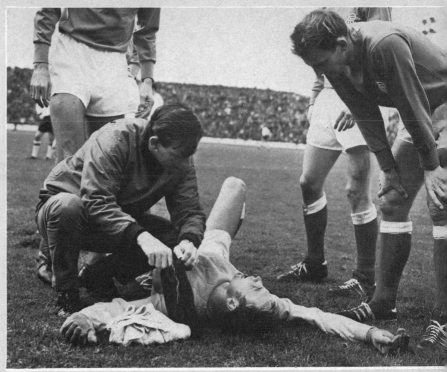

Soccer casualty report. Rangers' 'keeper Gerry Neef (above) gets treatment after being knocked out in a goalmouth clash. It's agony for Rangers' outside-right Willie Henderson (left) as he is helped off the field with a broken jaw. Another game is over for Joe McBride as he is lead away with blood streaming from a cut above his eye. Just three of the many casualties that football throws up every season.

When it comes to the CRUNCH

THE SECRET fear of every player – the nagging worry of injury.

Every tackle can bring disaster, every sudden change of direction can tear or strain a muscle or ligament and put a player out of football for months, or even end his career for ever.

In the tense, tough world of professional football you have got to have guts.

There is little room for any player to hide on the football field. The fans can always forgive a tryer, never a player who shirks a tackle or draws back from the challenge.

When it comes to the crunch, football is really a man's game.

IT'S A FACT of life in Scottish football that Rangers and Celtic dominate the game and, to some extent, the sports pages.

But at the start of last season in Scotland's exciting curtain raiser, the League Cup, two teams emerged from the ranks to snap angrily at the heels of the big guns.

The incentive, of course, was there from the start, when Rangers and Celtic were paired together in the same opening section. In fact it was Celtic who marched on at the Final at Hampden to win the trophy for the fifth time in a row – a magnificent record.

But the teams that brought real brightness to the scene were St. Johnstone, the losing finalists, and Ayr United, beaten by Celtic in the semis – but only after a replay.

In the first match Celtic drew 3-3 with Ayr when the most reasonable judges expected the part-time men to be well beaten. Celtic made no mistake in the second game which was watched by a crowd of 48,000, a tribute to the away Ayr had caught the imagination of the fans. They had already caused a shock

Celtic on the attack (above left) as Jimmy Johnstone beats three Airdrie defenders.

Celtic on defence as 'keeper John Fallon punches clear during an Ayr United attack.

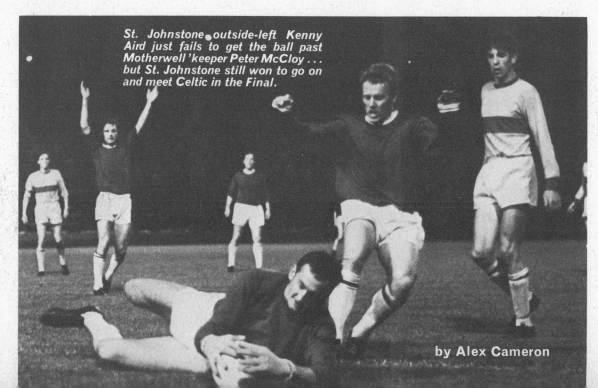

St. Johnstone outside-left Kenny Aird just fails to get the ball past Motherwell 'keeper Peter McCloy . . . but St. Johnstone still won to go on and meet Celtic in the Final.

by Alex Cameron

The Day Celtic Made History-Again!

Wallace under suspension, and Johnstone listed only as substitute, this was a big decision.

Although St. Johnstone had shocked Celtic by grabbing a draw at Parkhead in the League, they were slow to settle on the Hampden pitch.

While they were still finding their feet, Bertie Auld scored a wonder goal. Bertie's arms, held aloft in a victory "V", proved prophetic, for the goal was the only one of the game.

So ended a dream for St. Johnstone, but they, and all the other provincial clubs, must take tremendous credit for making the tournament a real money-spinner.

by beating Rangers in the League.

Ayr, in fact, went into the lead through Alex Ingram. But Harry Hood equalised, and in the second-half Steve Chalmers got the winner.

In the other semi, St. Johnstone had already knocked out Motherwell, and so the scene was set for a romantic final. The little side from the country against the mighty Celtic.

Before the kick-off, Jock Stein announced that Tommy Gemmell would not play – a disciplinary move because the left-back had been ordered off when playing for Scotland against Germany. With Lennox injured, and

The golden goal that won Celtic their fifth League Cup in a row. Berti Auld (top) slams a right foot shot into the net for the winning goal.

The game's over and won and now it's time for the happy Celts to fill the League Cup with some victory champagne. No wonder they look so happy!

MEET THE

WHILE £100,000 transfers are becoming almost common in the big-money English League, in Scotland they are still in their infancy.

In fact, Rangers striker Colin Stein is the only man to have been sold for the magical six-figure fee north of the border. But it has been money well spent as far as the Ibrox club is concerned.

Since joining them from Hibs, Colin has proved himself worth every penny of that fat transfer fee. His strong running, deadly accuracy around the goal, and amazing courage have made him one of Scotland's most feared attackers.

Colin fears no one, but defences tremble when they see the blond-headed Stein charging in on goal.

COLIN STEIN–Rangers

It's the type of goal that has made Colin Stein Scotland's highest priced player. Here he dives full length to head the ball past a surprised Kilmarnock defence to give Rangers two more valuable points.

GOAL GRABBERS

Determination and power, these have always been the secret of Joe McBride's amazing goal grabbing record, and here he shows just why he is one of the most feared men in football as he crashes an unsavable shot past Partick Thistle 'keeper George Niven.

JOE McBRIDE – Hibs.

HE HAS been called "The Man of Many Clubs" but Hibs star Joe McBride should really be called "The Man of Many Successes".

For with each of his seven senior clubs Joe has finished as top goal-scorer – a record unequalled by any top class player.

Think of the chunky centre and you think of goals, great goals, scored for teams throughout Britain. Joe's roll call of clubs reads: Kilmarnock, Wolves, Luton, Partick Thistle, Motherwell, Celtic and now Hibs.

But in all his travelling Joe has found that the most difficult centre-half to play against is Dundee United's Doug Smith. Says Joe: "Billy McNeill of Celtic is the best centre-half I have seen, yet I usually manage to have a good game against him. But Doug Smith is another matter; I never have much success with him."

Joe has had two highlights in his career. His first cap, against Wales in 1967, and his first medal, a League Cup winners when with Celtic.

Unachieved ambition? "I'd like a Scottish Cup medal, the only honour that I have still to get," says Joe.

17

Ayr United 'keeper David Stewart gets up early to stop Kilmarnock's Eddie Morrison heading home yet another classic goal.

EDDIE MORRISON - KILMARNOCK

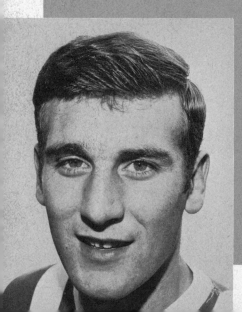

HE'S BIG. He's strong. He scores goals. In fact, Kilmarnock striker Eddie Morrison is almost the perfect example of the modern goal-getter.

The Killie man usually plays inside-right with Ross Mathie playing the twin striker role with him. Together they make one of the deadliest partnerships in the country.

Eddie went to Kilmarnock from Junior football and was an immediate sensation. In his first five games for the Ayrshire club he scored six goals – and he has been banging them in ever since.

Eddie's strongest feature is probably his heading ability. He gets tremendous height in his jumps, and power in his headers.

So far he has had no recognition from the Scotland selectors, but his ability must bring him honours soon.

SCOTLAND has long been famed for small, goal-getting inside-forwards and the latest to carry on the tradition is St. Johnstone's Henry Hall.

For the £15,000 they paid Stirling Albion, the Perth side obtained the bargain of the decade. In only his second season Henry smashed their goal-scoring record which had stood since before the last war, and he looks destined for even greater fame.

Although small, he shrugs off the hardest tackles and can outjump the tallest defender. Part of his fantastic fitness may lie in the fact that he is a physical training instructor in his spare time.

His greatest honour was his first appearance in a Scotland jersey when he came on as substitute for the Scottish League against the English League in March 1969.

Henry always finds playing against Cameron Murray of St. Mirren difficult. Says the St. Johnstone star: "His timing in the tackle is terrific, and he reads a game so well that you never get much room against him".

Henry's ambition now, apart from more honours for himself, is to take St. Johnstone into European football.

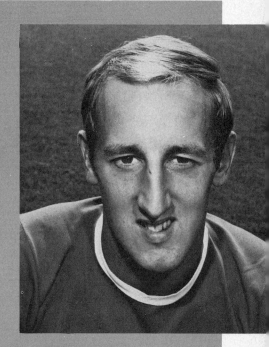

HENRY HALL - ST. JOHNSTONE

Small, quiet . . . but deadly. Meet St. Johnstone's Henry Hall, the man who last season shot his way to the top of Scotland's scoring list. Celtic left-half Jim Brogan gets a close-up view of the power shooting which has made Hall one of Scotland's most popular players.

The ability to make and take chances near goal has already won Gordon Wallace the title of Scotland's Footballer of the Year a few seasons ago. Now his sharp-shooting is helping to turn Dundee's forward line into one of the most dangerous in the First Division.

GORDON WALLACE – Dundee

THE PRIDE OF DUNDEE. That's Gordon Wallace, goal-scorer extraordinary for the Dens Park side.

It was a sad day for Raith Rovers' fans when the bustling centre left Starks Park – and no wonder! Gordon is the only player outside the "Old Firm" to have been awarded Scotland's Player of the Year trophy, the highest award that Scotland's top sports writers can give to a player. And how well it was earned. In season 1967-68 Raith looked set for the long drop into the Second Division. But a wonderful scoring burst by Wallace saved the Kirkcaldy team almost single-handedly.

Now Dundee thrills to the sharpness of the slightly-built Wallace – the sharp-shooter who is right on target.

"JAUNTY JOE" they call Aberdeen winger Joe Harper, because the little man always seems to be grinning and joking.

But opposing defences are not at all happy when facing this little box-of-tricks who is one of the best users of a "dead" ball in the country.

Joe sampled English football with Huddersfield in between two spells with Morton. He says: "The highlight of my career was signing for Aberdeen. I have always had an ambition to play for them."

But following it closely was his first Under 23s cap against Wales.

Now his ambition is more caps for himself and honours for the Dons. Both look a formality with this dynamic character around.

Joe's most difficult opponent is Pat Stanton, Hibs' classy wing-half. "He has everything that a top-class wing-half needs" says Joe. "He is the most difficult for me to get past. He is a really great player."

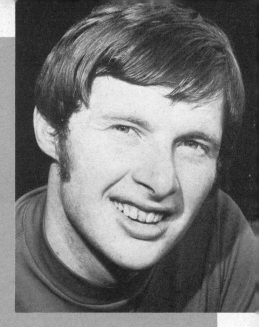

JOE HARPER – Aberdeen

Joe Harper is a little man with a big shot. He has the habit of making difficult things look easy and goalkeepers all over the country dread the thought of giving him even half a chance near goal.

Alan Gordon has taken the coolness and intelligence which has won a University Degree on to the pitch with him. Here he is outjumping Celtic centre-half Billy McNeill to head Dundee United into the lead at Parkhead.

ALAN GORDON - Dundee Utd.

ALAN GORDON, of Dundee United, is definitely one of Scotland's "brainiest" players and he has the certificates to prove it!

For Alan is the proud holder of an M.A. Degree which he gained at Edinburgh University. He intends to use the Degree when his playing days are over.

But the Dundee United fans are hoping this will not be for a long, long time yet. For since he joined the Tannadice side from Hearts, Alan has proved himself one of the most accomplished players to land at Tayside.

One of the country's most elegant inside-forwards, the tall, blond Gordon also packs a mighty shot.

H E'S SCOTLAND'S cricket-ing football player; or should it be Scotland's footballing cricket player?

Certainly Hearts star, Donald Ford qualifies for the All Rounder tag. When he is not grabbing the goals for Hearts, Donald wields a nifty bat for the West Lothian cricket side.

But it is as Hearts all-action centre-forward that Donald has really made his name in the world of sport.

He amazes everyone who plays against him. How can so much power and skill be packed into such a small package?

Donald feels that he could be even better if he weighed a little more than the ten stones which show when he stands on the scales.

"I have tried everything to put on weight" says the centre, "but nothing seems to work."

DONALD FORD - Hearts.

One of the hardest men to put off the ball is Hearts centre Donald Ford. Despite this determined tackle by Dundee United centre-half, Doug Smith, Ford still got through to score.

To earn a nickname such as "Dixie" you've got to know a lot about goal scoring. Motherwell centre John Deans has certainly earned that nickname with some tremendous goals over the past few seasons.

JOHN DEANS - Motherwell

THERE IS A NEW "Dixie" creating panic among defences, and like his illustrious namesake, who was such a big star with Everton, he is a goal-snatching centre-forward.

John Deans of Motherwell is living up to the nickname that delighted Fir Park supporters have given him, by producing some magical moments and great goals.

"Dixie" has not always been completely happy at Motherwell, but nothing has stopped the goal flair of this 23-year-old. He has a magnificent shot with either foot. Good in the air, John is a manager's dream centre-forward.

Signed from Neilston Juniors for £250, John is now worth at least 200 times this amount.

"WISPY" WALLACE gets his nickname from his quiet manner of speaking. But get this Celtic ace on the turf and he screams out for attention.

Willie is the one-man forward line. Put him back into midfield, and you will get a first class performance from one of Scotland's most exciting players.

He hustles and bustles about, and even when he is not scoring goals you can be sure that he is taking a big part in the making of them for his team-mates.

When Willie scored his 100th goal for Celtic, it was said that he could easily reach the double century.

Willie Wallace, the action man they call "Wispy" is now well on his way to doing just that.

WILLIE WALLACE - Celtic

Willie Wallace has often been described as the most professional in Scottish football. He can play anywhere and make a great job of it but there is no hiding his favourite role of striker. Here you see just how much he enjoys the job of goal scoring as he slams the ball over Dundee United 'keeper Donald McKay.

IT SEEMS STRANGE that Celtic and Rangers should be the spear-head of the Scottish challenge in Europe. When we look back to the beginnings of this new era we realise that it was Hibs that had enough vision to pioneer the glamorous road to the Continental clashes that we know today.

Yet, back in 1955 when the European Cup became the first Continental trophy to be competed for, Hibs was the one British team to go forward.

This was excitingly different, which the visionaries at Easter Road realised. It didn't take the rest of the country too long to see that Hibs had been right. The semi-final appearance which brought Rheims, the famous French club, to Edinburgh was enough to convince every fan that a brave new soccer world had been opened up. The skill of legendary French forward ace Raymond Kopa was paraded against Hibs, and the Scots' team failed to make the final. Rheims, of course, were beaten by what was then a practically unknown Spanish team – Real Madrid.

The Spaniards were to set up their own legend, clinging to the coveted European Cup trophy for five years and building to the peak of perfection we saw at Hampden in the 1960 Final.

If Hibs had opened the floodgates for European football in Britain, then the epic Hampden Park clash between Real Madrid and Eintracht Frankfurt of West Germany, hammered home the fact that the British Isles could not stand aloof while football of this standard was being played across Europe.

Our Scottish champions, Rangers, had been humbled by Eintracht by 12 goals to 4 in the two leg semi-final and Eintracht were hammered 7-3 by the magnificent Spanish side.

Real's forward line can never be forgotten. It read: Canario, Del Sol, Di Stefano, Puskas and Gento – every one a world star. And at Hampden the two greatest stars, Argentina's Alfredo Di Stefano and Hungary's Ferenc Puskas, shared the 7 goals. Puskas, the tubby inside-forward, nicknamed the "Galloping Major", scored 4 while the elegant, almost aristocratic Di Stefano made a fantastic hat-trick.

A few months later Scotland was priviliged to have a first look at an up-and-coming Portuguese team, Benfica, who defeated Hearts in the first round. A Benfica team which contained that commanding, impressively-bearded centre-half Germano, and the gloriously talented midfield ace Coluna. They went on to win the Cup and repeated the feat the following year when Eusebio broke through into their team and into the glittering history of the top European torunament.

The pattern remained the same. New names. New teams. New stars. I saw Dundee fight their way to the semi-final the following year and "discovered" the then unknowns, Karl-Heinz Schnellinger, the West German defender who was then

European Cup

Cup Winners' Cup

Fairs Cup

MAGIC CHALLENGE

Here are just some of the many great players which European football has brought to the Scottish public. Above, left to right: Ferenc Puskas, Real Madrid; Eusebio, Benfica; Gianni Rivera, A.C. Milan. Below: Luis Suarez, Inter Milan.

with Cologne, the frail and magical midfield ace Gianni Rivera of AC Milan, and the world-rated Belgian, Paul Van Himst of Anderlecht.

Then, when Rangers met Inter-Milan, we found out about Helenio Herrera and his feared defensive system "cattanaccio", and we saw the first "sweeper", Armando Picchi, and the artistic genius of Inter's Luis Suarez.

Inter established themselves and their defensive philosophy as the twin powers of European football for several years until, finally, they were beaten by a team committed to attack, by a team who had never played in the European Cup before, by a team no one outside of Scotland had rated. By Celtic.

The Celtic team, reconstructed by Jock Stein, went to Lisbon on that May afternoon in 1967 as under-dogs. No team from Britain had ever won the European Cup. Not only that, no team had ever broken the grip that the Latin countries had held on the trophy since it began more than ten years before.

But Stein's men did it. They beat Inter-Milan 2-1, with goals coming from Tommy Gemmell their extrovert, attacking full-back, and from their centre-forward Steve Chalmers. It was an outstanding achievement and Celtic, with an all-Scottish eleven, still remains the only team to win the Cup using only their own national players.

by Ken Gallacher

A day Celtic will never forget — it's the European Cup Final in Lisbon against Inter Milan. It looks as though centre Steve Chalmers has scored . . . but somehow Inter 'keeper Sarti managed to stop the ball on the line. But there was no stopping Celtic and they went on to become the first British team to win the Cup.

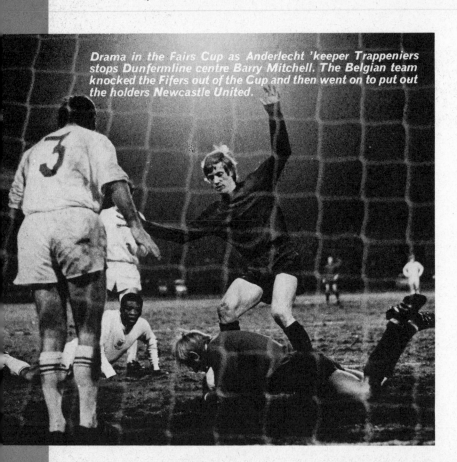

Drama in the Fairs Cup as Anderlecht 'keeper Trappeniers stops Dunfermline centre Barry Mitchell. The Belgian team knocked the Fifers out of the Cup and then went on to put out the holders Newcastle United.

Throughout the 60s the other two European tournaments grew in strength, too. Twice Rangers reached the final of the European Cup Winners' Cup – and twice they lost.

The last time was in the same year as Celtic's triumph in Lisbon, when we again watched a rising generation of European stars. In the Bayern Munich team, which beat them by the only goal of the game, were the smooth and immaculate Franz Beckenbauer and the Continent's ace chance-snapper Gerd Muller. Two years later both players were to appear in the West German team which stopped Scotland reaching the World Cup Finals in Mexico.

The Fairs Cup began as very much the poor relation tournament, and then suddenly exploded into a money-spinning competition which attracted outstanding

A TALE OF TWO COINS

IT WAS a March night in 1967 that I first saw a major European tournament settled by the toss of a coin.

It was at the Romareda Stadium in Spain, when Rangers met Real Saragossa in the quarter-final of the European Cup Winners' Cup. Rangers went to Spain with a two goal lead, but Saragossa levelled scores with a last-minute penalty, which sent the game into extra time.

Rangers dominated that extra half hour and Dave Smith missed a penalty for them. That meant the toss of a coin was needed to separate the teams.

From the Press Box we watched as the referee Michel Kitabjian from France called the two captains, John Greig and the Spanish left-back Reija, together before sending the silver coin arching upwards, spinning and shining in the glare of the floodlights. The wind blew the coin away from the little group and they raced towards it – suddenly Greig was dancing round the field and Willie Henderson was turning cartwheels. Rangers were through to the semi-finals!

Later Greig told me: "It was the worst moment of my life. Twice in the game, at the start of the match and then at the start of extra time, I had called correctly. I didn't think it was possible for it to happen again."

Both Greig and the then Rangers Manager Scot Symon criticised this method of settling such an important tie. Said Symon: "The time to criticise is when you have won in this way."

The second time a coin was used to settle a game was when Celtic met Benfica in an epic European Cup game.

Celtic had gone to Lisbon and were winning 3-0; they looked certain of reaching the third round of the tournament. Somehow it didn't work out that way – Benfica levelled the scores at 3-3 in the final seconds of the game! It came so late that no one knew at first whether the goal had beaten the final whistle or not – but the score still remained the same after extra time.

This time, as pandemonium reigned in the Estadio de Luz, the Dutch referee Laurens van Raavens took the rival captains Billy McNeill and Benfica's Mario Coluna into his dressing room. There he made them toss the coin twice, once to decide who should call, and again to decide the result of the game. Billy McNeill won each time, to everyone's amazement, and Celtic went on to meet the Italian champions Fiorentina.

Again, though, the Scots were not happy at this method of deciding games. Said Celtic boss Jock Stein: "After two games, two great games, it was a tragedy that one of us should go out like that."

Celtic went further than merely criticising the coin-tossing business in public – the club sent a formal letter of complaint to the Union of European Football Associations suggesting that this way of settling games should be scrapped.

teams from all over Europe.

It also gave the provincial teams a chance to play against the top teams – as well as providing the "Old Firm" with a third entrance into Europe! Kilmarnock has been able to meet Eintracht, Everton, and Leeds United; Dunfermline has faced up to Atletico Bilbao, Saragossa, and Spartak Brno of Czechoslovakia; Hibs has faced Roma, Barcelona, and Hamburg; and Celtic and Rangers have had epic matches, Celtic against Barcelona, and Rangers against Leeds United and Bilbao.

It's a goal Rangers almost got in their European Cup Winners' game against Steaua. Jim Baxter just fails to get his foot to a cross from Colin Stein. The Ibrox team won but lost in the next round to Gornik of Poland.

Bobby Calder

WHO IS the most valuable person in Scottish soccer today? Fans will argue that Jock Stein, Jimmy Johnstone, Colin Stein and Peter Cormack each has a claim to that distinction – but I doubt if any of the boys who know the Scottish soccer scene inside-out, would agree.

Most of them would plump for a small, dapper, balding man in his sixties whose name is known and respected by every soccer official, – both minor and senior – in Scottish football, Aberdeen's chief representative, Bobby Calder.

For Calder, a former top-grade referee is truly the man with the £1,000,000 eyes.

In his 21 years with Aberdeen he has brought the club almost 3 to 4 million pounds in transfer fees for players he has discovered, and he is rightly considered to be Britain's top soccer prospector.

Significantly two out of the four really big money transfers in Scottish soccer during the past year have been Calder "discoveries".

Within a few months, Aberdeen transferred Jimmy Smith and Tommy Craig to Newcastle United and Sheffield Wednesday respectively for £100,000 each – only two of the well dressed little Glasgow man's top discoveries.

Both Smith and Craig cost the Dons only a signing-on-fee, thanks to the persuasion and sharp eye of Calder.

Calder reckons that his ability to spot a future star so quickly stems from his refereeing days. He says: "I refereed every type of match during my career. I watched youngsters through school, juvenile, senior and international competitions and it was there I got the knack of spotting players.

"As a referee one could easily spot the lads with talent, and usually the ones I picked out in the minor grades did make it later on as top professionals.

"I was in charge of matches all over the world – South America included – and I soon learned that talent can be spotted quickly.

"When I quit refereeing in

The Man With The £ 1,000,000 Eyes

Jimmy Smith was spotted as a junior, taken to Aberdeen, and then transferred to Newcastle United for £100,000.

by Bob Patience

30

1948, Aberdeen offered me the post of chief representative and I jumped at the chance. Since then I have watched a lot of great footballers come and go, but I must say I still enjoy picking them out just as much as ever.

"Some of the youngsters of today are brilliant. It's true there were a lot of fine players in my day but I don't agree they were any better than today's youngsters.

"Some of the lads I have signed would have stood out a mile in some of the great teams of twenty or thirty years ago. You cannot ignore talent. If it is there then it will shine through, and players like Jimmy Smith, Tommy Craig and Doug Fraser – just three of the lads I took to Pittodrie would have been as big stars then as they are today.

"And our present players are much more dedicated and faster than the players of that era. It's true the cash incentive is greater now, but most of our young players thrive on hard work and they are certainly much quicker off the mark than players used to be.

"In those days a player would have time to beat one, two, or even three players, look about and then part with the ball. Now a player must beat a man quickly, part with the ball, and then find space for the return pass in half the time players used to have.

"I would never criticise present day players. I think they are the hardest workers the game has ever known.

"A player can have a lot of inborn talent, but if he does

He has been a hero with Aberdeen, Dundee and Chelsea ... but Charlie Cooke remembers when Calder signed him for Aberdeen.

not have the intelligence or courage to back it up then he is useless to a club.

"I have watched a lot of youngsters who, with a bit of brainwork, could be first class players. But there are too many of them who just cannot pick up what is required. It's not enough to have good ball control or the ability to head or kick a ball. A good player thinks football. He knows when to move into an open space for a return pass, when to part with a ball, and when to shoot or cross.

"This is an inbred talent – no amount of teaching will improve a youngster who does not have it. I've seen many boys look good in practice but when it comes to an actual match their failings soon show up.

"And, of course, courage is a must nowadays. The nature of present day football puts an emphasis on the physical side of the game and the best ball worker in

Tommy Craig, another of Calder's £100,000 discoveries.

the world is of little use to anyone if he is afraid.

"This is one of the reasons for Scots doing so well in England. I believe Scots have that extra little 'dig' and that extra bit of heart which goes hand-in-hand with a top class player. That's the reason why so many of our boys make it down south."

THE LONGEST DAY

by Pat Stanton, Hibs.

As far as I'm concerned, football's a great life, one I wouldn't change – except for one thing. I'd love to be on a winning side every week.

It's an impossible dream, I know, but to my mind that's the way every professional footballer should feel about the game. My life is geared to match day. And I feel that's the way it should be. After all, match days are the most important in any player's life.

I try to let nothing upset me or distract me before a match. A moment's loss of concentration during a game can mean a goal for your opponents. And as a defender, that's one thing that annoys me more than anything.

On match Saturdays I have a set routine that rarely varies. Depending on how far I have to travel I usually rise between 9 and 10 a.m. – never earlier.

I never have breakfast in bed. I just cannot enjoy a meal in bed, and certainly not on match day. I always wash and shave leisurely before sitting down to breakfast – I eat the same thing every morning; cereal with milk and sugar, a little toast and a couple of cups of coffee.

I take my time, and try to relax over the coffee, thinking little about the game ahead. I leave that until nearer the kick-off time when I'm with the rest of the lads.

If we are playing at home, I leave my house in Lasswade about 11 a.m. and take my wife to her mother's home before meeting up with the rest of the team at an Edinburgh hotel for lunch. My routine is always the same. The meal never changes. Some of the lads have steak, others a salad. I always have chicken. There's a strict ruling about potatoes. No potatoes!

Afterwards we are allowed some tea and toast. Nothing else. Before the bus leaves for the ground we have half an hour or so to relax in the hotel lounge. Some of the boys sit and read, but most of us watch television.

I find that watching the lunch-time sports programmes relaxes me before the game. I've heard of players who are ice-cool and calm, with no sign of nerves before a match. I've never met one. I've been in top class football a few seasons now, but I still feel the butterflies starting as the kick-off gets nearer.

When we are at home, it's a short bus trip to the ground, but travelling to away games it's harder to keep your mind off the game, to keep the tension down.

There's the inevitable sing-song, of course, and I always try to have a word of encouragement with some of the younger, less experienced lads in the team. This usually helps to calm my nerves as well as theirs.

I usually start to get ready for the game about 2.30 p.m. I don't think I'm superstitious but like most players, I've got a couple of whims about getting changed.

I always put my jersey on first, and I never wear white laces. It may sound ridiculous but I reckon they're too conspicuous. I'd hate to go out looking too bold, then proceed to turn in a poor performance.

Then comes the game itself, the object of all the training, planning, plotting, thinking. And afterwards, again like most players, my reactions vary with the result.

If we are beaten I usually find myself sitting for ages just staring at the wall and hurling my boots around. But if we've won, it's a different story.

I strip off as quickly as possible, leap into the bath and sing, laugh and joke with the lads. Afterwards a quick celebration drink with some of the boys, then out to pick up my wife, Margaret.

A win means a meal out, then back to watch the game on television. A defeat sees me moping about the house. I just can't bear to go out in a bad mood.

But then comes Sunday, and the excitement starts all over again. As I said earlier, it's a great life and I wouldn't change it – except to be on the winning side every week.

Billy McNeill. Celtic.

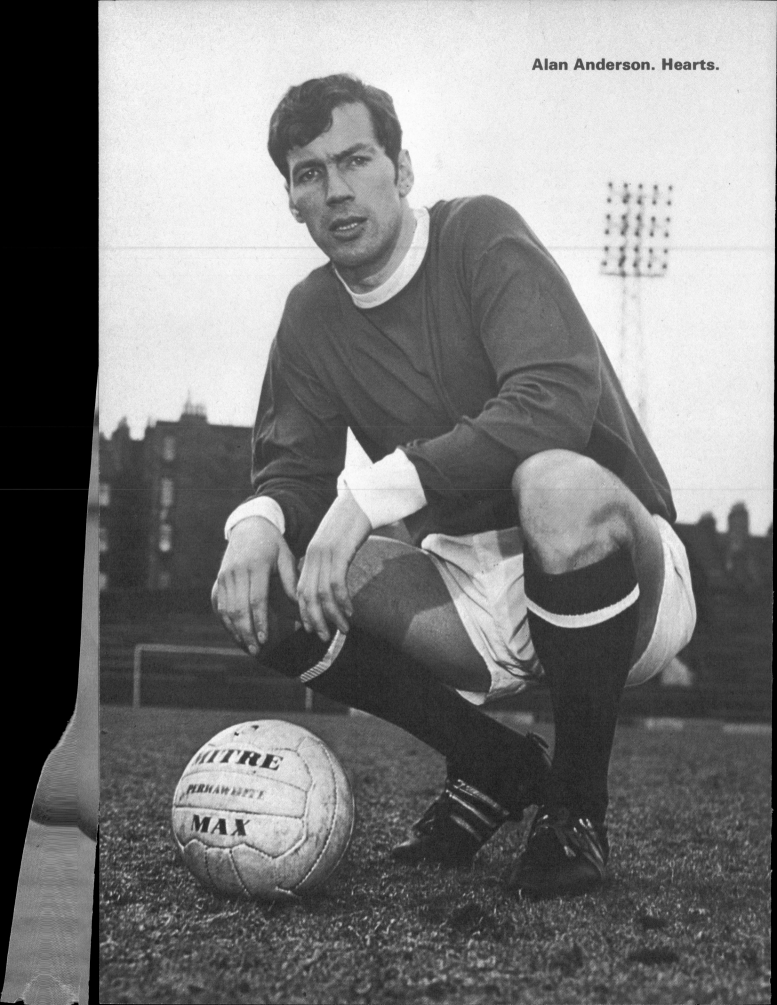

Alan Anderson. Hearts.

George McLean. Dunfermline.

Bertie Auld. Celtic.

Orjan Persson. Rangers.

Alex Edwards. Dunfermline.

OLD PLAYERS are supposed to sit back and polish their medals. I have no time for that, I'm too busy preparing Celtic to win more medals!

I'm no greybeard yet – I think I can still sprint on to the Park – but as a player who was in the Coronation Cup winning team and the side which captured the 1954 League and Cup double, I am sometimes amazed when I count up the changes in soccer.

I often wonder what the players who were around in 1948, when I was with my first senior club, Morton, would make of football life if they could take a peep at the behind-the-scenes preparations today.

There is one basic difference – players work far harder at training now than they ever did twenty years ago.

Take goalkeepers. They used to do the same sort of training as the outfield players, although it was completely unsuited to them. Now their training is specialised, to sharpen up their reflexes.

In fact, I reckon the 'keepers at Celtic Park do more in a morning now than used to be done in a month.

The training for the rest of our squad is basically the same, but we keep a very close watch on the "heavy squad" – that's the big men in the pool such as John Hughes, Bobby Murdoch, Billy McNeill and Tommy Gemmell.

There are times during the season when they have to be given more training than, say, the little lightweights, such as Jimmy Johnstone or Bobby Lennox.

This often happens when games are cancelled because of bad weather; the big fellows have to work

harder to make up for the lack of match practice.

Another major difference the old-timers would notice is the amazing amount of work done with the ball today.

Maybe you'll be surprised to hear it. After all, the game is called football – but an awful lot of training was done without a ball when I started as a trainer.

Now, apart from a few exercises, almost everything, even the sprints, is done with a football.

It all helps to make training interesting. The boring old system of nothing but lapping the track is finished for ever.

Players look forward to the training. We have practice matches almost every day, and believe me, they

FITNESS
...the key to success

by Neil Mochan, Celtic Coach

When Celtic players talk about being put through the hoop at training they're not kidding! Here manager Jock Stein makes sure Jim Brogan gets down to it.

are as keen as any league match.

I'm lucky. I've heard of trainers who have to bully their side. We never have to do that at Celtic.

The modern player is a real professional. He knows he has to work to get fit, and he does!

On the field the big difference must surely be the disappearance of individuality although I don't think this applies so much to the top teams. Think of Manchester United and you think of George Best. Think of Celtic and you think of Jimmy Johnstone or John Hughes. Yet although individual stars, each one has to have scope inside a team plan. It has to be that way – for even great solo stars need help to beat the counter-marking by which every opposing team tries to trap forwards.

One of the greatest individuals I have ever seen was Charlie Tully.

How would Charlie manage today? The simple test is that a good footballer from any time could succeed in modern football, and Charlie was a good footballer.

Of course he would have problems to overcome. Charlie liked to juggle the ball, and a pack of modern defenders might change that.

Sometimes he played with his tongue as much as his head.

I don't think modern referees have any sense of humour, so that would be a difficulty.

Today players have to work for their big salaries. Fans who say that it is easy money just don't know what they are talking about.

I don't regret missing the big money era, and I think it's pointless for anyone who played twenty years ago to have regrets. How can you?

Keep them busy – that's the Celtic training motto. Tommy Gemmell (above) leads the way over some hurdles while (below) Jock Stein gives 'keeper John Fallon a special work-out in goal.

Nobody has yet found a way of turning the clock back, or forward!

I was paid well enough by the standards of that time and although today's wage packets may seem inflated to the players of my day, I can assure you that they are well earned.

Footballers today talk more about football, think more about football, and work harder at their football.

Few fans realise the punishment that a modern player has to take in a match. Certainly it's different from twenty years ago when full-backs used to charge in with sliding tackles and any referee could see that.

But now it's different. There are players who are amongst the best actors in the business, rolling over dramatically to make quite a simple foul seem a major incident.

Star players have opponents detailed to mark them throughout a game, and sometimes they are not too particular how it is achieved.

What can be more frustrating than to be shadowed, and perhaps unfairly, at every move? Many teams operate to such a plan; no wonder the retaliation crime rate rises.

I believe that the general all-round standard of football has improved, but I regret – and I reckon the fans will agree with me – the disappearance of the personalities from some of our teams.

This has not happened to the top sides. They have been able to cream off the top talent, to build up the box-office names.

But the smaller clubs are caught in a vicious circle.

They have had to sell off most of their big names through the years – players who could not easily be replaced.

Some have tried, and successfully, to compensate by improved team planning. But I still feel it is big names that the fans want to see and too often this is lacking.

That's why I believe that the Celtic and Rangers monopoly will expand even more during the coming years. They are the only clubs who can really afford to put into action what other sides may want to try.

There is no secret about the success formula at Celtic Park. From the manager down, everyone has grafted to make sure that we were successful.

Celtic was always rated a fit team, but in recent seasons we have added extra ingredients of skill and especially experience.

The players were disheartened with being second best. They realised that if they did knuckle down to their work they could win honours – and Jock Stein supplied the leadership.

He is a perfect example of the modern track-suited manager. The old divisions of managers who saw players only a few times a week, and took no active part in the

training, have disappeared.

The younger managers have changed all that. Nowadays the boss spends as much time with his players as anywhere else, supervising their training, and their tactics talks.

It means a different kind of tension for them, too. Now they are on the touchline instead of remotely watching the match from a directors box.

The tension communicates to the dug-out where the manager, trainer and substitutes sit. I have never felt more nervous than at the semi-final of the European Cup against Dukla Prague in Czechoslovakia.

We had a 3-1 lead from the first leg, and we were closer than ever before to something no British club had ever achieved – a place in the European Cup Final.

The manager's tactics were all-out defence, with only Steve Chalmers up front. It is something we had not done before, and are unlikely to repeat.

But I really sweated on the bench that day. So near, and yet so far, but it all worked out well with a 0-0 draw. And of course eventually the final – and the European Cup!

Big John Hughes and Willie Wallace (above) show how grim a modern weight training session can be, while (below) full-back Jim Craig is left to solve his own little problem in another part of the Celtic commando course.

IT IS THE JOB every football fan would love – managing his favourite team. Maybe it is the dream of winning the Cup, or the thrill of challenging the major leagues in Europe, or maybe it is simply that the manager is a fan himself and wants only one thing – to make his team the greatest.

Nowadays a club is a complex organisation with a large staff of players and backroom boys, – and somebody has got to be boss! This is the manager's job and it keeps changing just as surely as the date on the calendar. A lot of people say that there is nothing new in football; all I can say is that a lot of the old team tactics have had a few facelifts in my time.

But basically a Scottish fan likes his soccer served up hot; he likes excitement, goals, and a physical type of game that makes some of the Latin countries shudder. As a soccer nursery, Scotland is second to none

Willie Waddell's first day as Rangers' manager and the players certainly seem to be pleased with the appointment.

Someone Has To Be Boss

by Willie Waddell, Rangers Manager

Hibs' manager Willie McFarlane gets away from his desk to take part in a training session. It looks as if he hasn't forgotten how to tackle.

although too often we allow English clubs to take our young stars down south.

But now most Scottish clubs have their own youth policies and every season fresh new faces appear in every team. The day of the soccer 'Babe' is here to stay.

Look at any first team pool, and you will find a youngster in the squad who is holding down a first, or making some established star fight to keep his place. This continued rivalry for a first team place has been a great boost for Scottish football in recent years. At Ibrox, and at many other grounds, our soccer apprentices know that a first team place is there for the taking, and it is a great encouragement to a manager to see how hard the youngsters are working at the game, and how dedicated and professional they are becoming.

Football is now a more demanding profession than ever before, it is faster, tougher and much more thoughtful.

There is still nothing more exciting and thrilling than to watch a brilliant individual on the move, and there will always be a place in football for the star. But more and more he has to curb some of his natural flair, his inspired burst of individualism, to play his part in the overall team plan. Football is meant as a team game today it is more important than ever to have men ready to slog into a set pattern, and more and more it is vitally important to have a team behind a team.

Trainers, coaches, scouts, physiotherapists, public relations staff; all help the manager for his most important task – the winning of matches. The day of the desk bound manager is over, it is now the turn of the tracksuit

It's Jock Stein, goalkeeper, as the Celtic boss shows his players how it should be done.

boss. It's not enough for a manager, trainer, or coach to ask his men to do something, he must be prepared to show by example. It's not enough to name a team and lay down a plan for them to follow, a manager must know his players, know their limitations and never ask them to do a

job that they are not equipped to do. You can talk, discuss, plan to the last detail, but it is on the park that the real work must be done. That is when a manager's right-hand becomes so important. It is on the field that the team captain must take over, that is why it is so vital for a club to have the right type of man for captain. Rangers have had a long line of famous skippers and John Greig must stand as equal to any. He, more than any player, has shown just what makes an ideal captain. Where the action is hottest you will find John urging all his team-mates, shielding the younger players, encouraging all the lads who are out of form. The manager must be boss in his club, the captain must always be boss on the field. Football today can offer a great life for the youngster, in return it demands all out effort, dedication, and a determination to keep the game of football as the greatest sport in the world.

Willie Waddell leads away during some sprint training. Left to right: Willie Johnston, Alex McDonald, Waddell, John Greig, Assistant Manager Willie Thornton, and Dave Smith.

PUNCH - UP

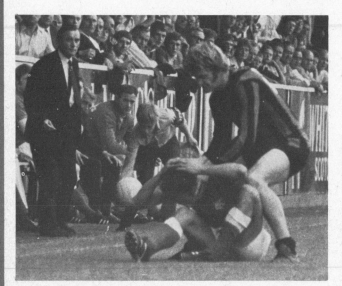

It's supposed to be a friendly match between Rangers and Queen's Park Rangers, but Rodney Marsh doesn't look very friendly as he wrestles with Rangers right-back Kai Johansen. (Left) The linesman, a coach, even a fan try to hold back Marsh as he tries to kick Johansen. (Right)

As Johansen receives treatment the enraged Marsh gets into more trouble as he butts Rangers' inside-right Bobby Watson.

Below: Trouble during the "Old Firm" match between Rangers and Celtic. Goalkeeper Gerry Neef lies injured after a tackle by Celtic's inside-right Bobby Lennox. Referee Tom Wharton races up to the scene as the angry Rangers surround Lennox.

Bottom: Referee Wharton has got to use all his 6' 4" and 15 stone to separate the players and get the game restarted . . . meanwhile Neef still lies injured as the players seem to think more about fighting than football.

I T IS A CURIOUS TRUISM that Scottish football could not have existed as we know it without the staggering tally of cash – close on £100,000,000 – which has poured in as the result of the steady exodus of soccer talent across the border.

And yet had this reservoir of lolly not been available to clubs, the game in Scotland might well have been given a much needed shake-up long ago.

The trek south by great and not-so-great players has been a disservice to spectators, but it is now so common that it is accepted as inevitable; anyway, the gap is usually filled in time.

At best the value of the tartan brain-drain has been arguable. This should not prevent us admiring the superb talents of Scots we can no longer see at home.

Who, in fact, has been Scotland's finest export to England?

The cheapest must certainly be Denis Law. He left Aberdeen for Huddersfield when he was only 15 and looked such unlikely athletic material – he wore glasses at the time – that none of the official reception committee picked him out.

But Law was to blossom under the dynanism of manager Bill Shankly and he finally arrived at Old Trafford via Torino after a short spectacular spell in Italian football.

Sir Matt Busby paid £115,000 for him and football clubs throughout Europe were aghast. The gates were thus opened for a series of £100,000 transfer fees.

Law has certainly repaid his fee. Busby is the first to say so with a note of pride in his voice. Law's quick thinking and instant reflex reaction to the most unusual situation

THE GREAT

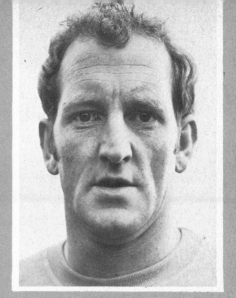

Far left: Ian Ure, Manchester United.

Second left: Bobby Hope, West Brom.

Below left: Denis Law, Manchester United.

Left: Bobby Moncur, Newcastle United.

Right: Sandy Brown, Everton.

Below: Peter Marinello, Arsenal.

Bottom: Ron Yeats, Liverpool.

SOCCER BRAIN DRAIN

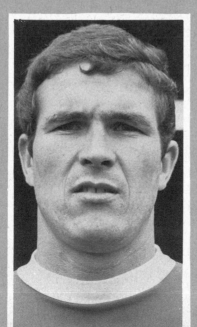

have made him a player apart.

The most controversial were Ian Ure and Alan Gilzean. Ure went to Arsenal and then to Manchester United. Gilzean went to Spurs, despite the fact that Sunderland made him a personal cash offer which would have set him up nicely for the future.

Bob Shankly was the Dens Park manager at the time. He resisted both transfers to the bitter end, even after much discussion and bewildering arguments. It was obvious though, that the players and the big-money clubs who wanted them would have to win.

In their years in the south, Ure and Gilzean have been a credit to Scotland. And "Gillie" has returned to Hampden several times to score some magnificent goals for our national team.

The most unsuccessful has been Jim Baxter, even though, in his best form, he has been the cleverest

wing-half I have ever seen.

Baxter went to Sunderland for £70,000 after having been on the Rangers transfer list for two years. But he never fitted in at Roker Park and he moved on to Nottingham Forest for £100,000.

He was there for less than two years when Forest made the most remarkable decision ever about such a highly-valued player. They gave him a free transfer!

Even Baxter, who thrived on the unexpected, was taken aback by this sudden drop to rock bottom on the "Soccer Stock Exchange".

Scotland is quick to recognise a bargain. Hearts tried to sign Baxter but opposition from Rangers was too great. So Jim landed back at Ibrox where it all began for him after a transfer from Raith Rovers for £17,500.

The most surprising were the £100,000 deals for Jimmy Smith and Tommy Craig. Smith went from Aberdeen to Newcastle and Craig, then

by Alex Cameron

an 18-year-old, moved to Sheffield Wednesday.

It was doubtful if they were suitable for the fast, tough hurly-burly of the game south of the border ... or so we thought at the time.

Smith at Pittodrie was a personality, brilliant on the ball and a great reader of play. But he was also prone to become involved with referees and his performance for English First Division soccer was suspect.

Craig had not long finished his apprenticeship and it was difficult to understand the £100,000 assessment. In fact, he was still in the Scots professional youth side.

Neither Newcastle nor Sheffield regrets spending the cash. And that is the only yardstick which counts.

The happiest are probably at Anfield. Ron Yeats, Ian St. John and Tommy Lawrence hero-worship their manager, Bill Shankly.

He, in turn, will not hear of any player with another team being suggested as better. Shankly is a fierce admirer of all things Scots – and particularly footballers.

The most unexpected move was Charlie Cooke's quick up-and-off to Chelsea from Dundee. He was bought from Aberdeen for £40,000 and looked as though he would settle at Dens Park.

But Tommy Docherty was looking for a personality for Stamford Bridge. So Charlie, the Darlin' of Dens, went to London.

A lot of truly great Scots – like Law – went south for the price of a rail ticket. Men such as Frank McLintock, who finally went to Arsenal on a big-money transfer from Leicester; Billy Bremner, Eddie Gray and Peter Lorimer, of Leeds United; Francis Burns and John Fitzpatrick, of Manchester

They both left Scotland as unknown schoolboys to join Leeds United, and now their names are known wherever football is played. Peter Lorimer (right) comes from Dundee and is reckoned to have the hardest shot in English football, while Billy Bremner (below) not only captains Leeds but also the Scottish International team, which is only right for a lad who was born at Bannockburn.

Eddie Gray, shows off some of his ball skill.

Pat Crerand left Celtic and joined Manchester United for a fee of £50,000 . . . you won't find a United fan who doesn't think that he wasn't a great bargain.

Alan Gilzean lines up for a shot, and it was his shooting ability which lead Tottenham Hotspur to sign him from Dundee.

United; Bob McKinlay, of Nottingham Forest; Bobby Moncur, of Newcastle United.

There are many others coming through like Willie Carr, of Coventry, and John O'Hare, of Derby County.

The most abrupt move was Peter Marinello's £100,000 shift from Hibs to Arsenal. He went straight into the Highbury side to score a goal in his first match against Manchester United.

Marinello was only 19. He was, and still is, a shy young man and the bright lights of London and the big money dazzled but didn't daze him.

He was the first youngster ever to walk into Highbury with long hair and not to be told to have it cut.

There are a lot of names I have missed out of my list. I hope none will be offended for it would be a crush to include them all.

So far I have dodged my opening question. But here goes . . .

The finest export is an honour shared by Dave Mackay and Pat Crerand.

Mackay's claim is obvious. He went from Hearts to Spurs for £27,500, an all-time bargain. Mackay inspired Spurs. He became a legend at White Hart Lane in his own time. And there have been genuine misgivings about his transfer to Derby County where he has again proved a superb leader.

No player has ever demonstrated determination more clearly. He defied defeat, chest out and chin jutting.

Off the pitch Mackay has been a credit to sport. He is exemplary, a man every youngster would like to emulate – but few ever will.

Crerand is much the same type as Mackay. A Gorbals boy who has written his own

story into the history of Manchester United.

Of course, there have been better players at Old Trafford and Crerand would be the first to say so.

But when he moved from Celtic for £50,000 he had to fashion his play into an unorthodox set-up in which every name around him was a household word.

Crerand became the chief engineer in midfield. His long raking passes searched out players like Law and Best.

Pound for £ it is my opinion that Mackay and Crerand have been the greatest. It is your privilege to argue.

Football can be grim even in Scotland, where the great game is so well loved. But the fan likes a laugh. And that he gets on Saturdays in the famous Daily Record "Sportsbag" column.

PICK OF THE 'SPORTSBAG'

This is probably the most popular column in sport, a column in which readers really have their say. That Hugh Taylor knows only too well. For 'Sportsbag' is conducted by our No. 1 sports writer. And it's quite a job!

For "Sportsbag" letter-writers pull no punches, telling the world just what they think about the game – and, especially, what they think about Taylor.

But Taylor is not a sitting duck. He hits back just as hard.

And so "Sportsbag", grave, gay authoritative, ferocious, facetious, humorous, angry, is the most entertaining column of all. Because it is never dull – as these examples from recent "Sportsbag" columns show . . .

Footballers should be like soldiers – neat and tidy on parade. There's no place for the long-haired lads on the soccer field.

So says D. Armour of Giffnock, Renfrewshire, who writes:

"Footballers should set an example to the youngsters of today. After all, they are the modern idols.

"But too many are hairy twits. They should have a year in the army. That would teach them. I don't see how anyone can play football with hair in his eyes. They'd feel better and play better if they were a little more tidy.'

● *You may have a point – but this reminds me of the story of the manager of a struggling Scottish club who was interviewing a young player.*

He told him severely: "Look, lad, if you're going to join us, you'll have to get your hair cut. We don't like hippy types at our club".

Said the player: "Ach, wait a minute, sir, it's the modern trend. And look at George Best wi' his long hair."

Said the manager sarcastically: "And can you play like George Best?"

The player: "Don't be daft. If I could play like George Best, do you think I'd want to join your lot?"

Celtic and Rangers . . . Rangers and Celtic . . . these big clubs are seldom out of "Sportsbag".

And there was one letter from D. McGrory, of Stirling, which, soon after Rangers had fired manager David White, said:

"Rangers are the daftest club in the country. They should never have put the blame on White. Can't they see beyond their own noses?

"What they should have done is offered Celtic's Jock Stein £100,000 tax free and a villa on the Riviera. No, not to become the manager . . . but to quit the country.

"Jock is Rangers' big trouble. If he hadn't been manager of Celtic, Rangers would still have been on top of the heap in Scotland."

● *Just shows how little you know . . . Jock prefers a bungalow in Paradise.*

A complaint about too many women going to football matches came from S. Jones of Bathgate. He wrote: "Football is a man's game. We like to let off steam and we don't want women around when a game's on. Women's place is in the house. They don't understand football, anyhow. Let them go to the pictures and Bingo – but keep away from the fitba'."

● *That reminds me of the Celtic supporter whose wife complained to him as he was off again to an away game . . . "You swine, you think more of Celtic than you do of me."*

To which he replied: "Huh,

by Hugh Taylor

SOCCER LAUGH-IN

I think more of Rangers than I do of you . . ."

Referees at the famous 'Old Firm' matches are always being criticised, especially in 'Sportsbag'.

Wrote P. Allan, of Stirling: "I think it is high time a foreign referee controlled the Celtic-Rangers game. There is too much bitterness for a home official to have the responsibility.

"Even our top officials are criticised by the clubs. It isn't fair. So let us go abroad for a man who will not be upset by the undercurrents and can't be blamed by either club for having bias."

● Bias at an 'Old Firm' game . . . What about the Ne'erday game when two fans had been celebrating. At the interval one said: 'Hey Tam, hoo aboot giving the referee a dram oot yer bottle?'

'Not on your life,' said the other, 'he'll see two teams in the second half.'

...AND A GUY CALLED ROD

THE EYES OF THE WORLD ARE UPON YOU..."

'I think he's forgotten it's an own goal'

'Willie – you can come out now Roy Barry has been transferred to England'

'When Pele scored his 1,000th goal they carried him round the field – alive!'

Ernie McGarr, Aberdeen goal-keeper who shot his way into the international reckoning in his first season as a first team player.

Dick Malone, Ayr United right back is one of the most attack conscious of Scotland's young full-backs. The 21-year old has already won an Under 23 cap and it looks as if there are many more on the way.

Sam Hastings, Clyde winger, has become a great favourite with the Shawfield fans since he signed from Hamilton Acas in 1964 for the bargain price of £5,000.

Willie Callaghan, Dunfermline right-back, is a great example of the great talent football can still supply to the First Division. Since joining the Fifers from Crossgates Primrose in 1960 Willie has gone on to be one of the best full-backs in the country.

Jim Cruickshank, Hearts goalkeeper, followed the long line of Queen's Park 'keepers who turned professional and quickly won international honours.

Eric Stevenson, Hibs outside-left, is one of the most talented ball players in the country. The amazing thing is that he joined Hibs as a free transfer man from their great Edinburgh rivals Hearts in 1960.

Tommy Gemmell, Celtic left-back, is the man with the hardest shot in Scottish football. He cost Celtic only £250 as a signing on fee from Junior club Coltness United in 1961. Since then he has been voted one of the best full-backs in the world.

Steve Murray, Aberdeen right-half. Steve joined Dundee in 1963 as a schoolboy and in his last season with Dundee missed only one game – the Scottish Cup semi-final against Celtic. Three days later he was signed by Aberdeen for £50,000.

Ian Mitchell, Dundee United inside-forward, came to Tannadice as a teenager with a great reputation. He had been a schoolboy cap and he quickly added youth caps and under-23-honours to his list.

SCOTTISH FOOTBALL WHO'S WHO IN SCOTT

Jackie McGrory, Kilmarnock centre-half, is a great example of the loyal club man. He joined Killie as a teenager in 1960 and next to Frank Beattie is the longest serving player at Rugby Park.

Bobby Collins, Morton inside-forward, is one of Scottish soccer's magic men. He was a star with Celtic, went to Everton and then moved to Leeds where Don Revie built his great team round him. He moved to Bury and then came back to Scotland in 1969 to join Morton.

Jackie McInally, Motherwell inside-forward, who joined them in 1967 from Kilmarnock for £5,000. Jackie has certainly repaid that transfer fee by helping to take Motherwell out of the Second Division and put them back in the position of being one of Scotland's attractive teams.

Ron McKinnon, Rangers centre-half, has followed a long line of Ibrox pivots into the Scottish national team. He is tremendously strong on the ground and seems to keep his best performances for the tough European competitions.

Dave Smith, Rangers wing-half, was one of Rangers' first big signings when he cost them £50,000 from Aberdeen in 1966. For a few seasons he struggled to find his real form but then slotted in to the role of sweeper to become one of the best in the country.

Ralph Brand, Raith Rovers inside-forward, was a great goal hero when with Rangers before he moved to Sunderland. At the start of last season Raith manager Jimmy Miller brought back his old team-mate to add experience to a young Starks Park side.

SH FOOTBALL   WHO'S WHO IN SCOTTISH FOO

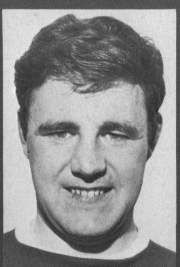

Benny Rooney, St. Johnstone centre-half, is the son of the Celtic physiotherapist, and was on Celtic's books as a teenager. He moved to Dundee United then joined Saints in 1966 for £5,000.

Cameron Murray, St. Mirren right-back, is a product of that well-known soccer nursery Drumchapel Amateurs. Although still a young man, he is the longest serving player on the Love St. books and one of the best full-backs in the country.

Sam Goodwin, Airdrie right-half, is one of soccer's strong men. One of the best tacklers in the business, Sam loves to join in the attack and his power play has made him one of the most sort after players in the first Division.

Scotland's 'keeper Jim Herriott safely clutches the ball as Treacy of Eire races in. Right-back Willie Callaghan covers up just in case.

St. Mirren 'keeper Jim Thorburn gets up high to punch clear from Dundee United's Kenny Cameron and his own wing-half Billy Fulton.

Dunfermline centre-half Doug Baillie is just too late with his tackle to stop Kilmarnock centre Ross Mathie firing in a shot. Kilmarnock out-side-right Tommy McLean follows up in case of a rebound.

Raith Rovers 'keeper Bobby Reid just gets his fingers to the ball as Dunfermline inside man Barry Mitchell smashes in a first-time shot.

Ayr United inside-right John Ferguson gets in a shot . . . but he just couldn't get it past Hibs goalkeeper Gordon Marshall who quickly got down to smother the ball.

Kilmarnock inside-right Eddie Morrison manages to get in a header despite an unusual tackle by Dunfermline centre-half Doug Baillie.

It's the goal that put Celtic into the Scottish Cup Final and outside-left Bobby Lennox makes no mistake as he crashes the ball into the empty net after Dundee 'keeper Alistair Donaldson had dropped the ball at his feet.

Dundee United full-back Stuart Markland outjumps team-mate Jim Cameron to head the ball clear during a St. Mirren attack. Standing by, just in case the United double act make any mistake, is St. Mirren outside-right Archie McCuaig.

THE CUP WIN THAT SHOOK THE WORLD

THEY SAID it could never happen, they said that it wouldn't happen . . . but Aberdeen still won the Scottish Cup on an April afternoon which proved that Soccer hadn't lost its magic.

Never before had a Cup Final looked so one-sided. Just how could Aberdeen, a middle of the league side, offer any real challenge to Celtic, the team of all the talents, League and League Cup winners for the fifth year in succession.

The men who cannot afford to be wrong, the bookmakers, had listed Aberdeen as 6-1 shots, odds that looked as if the money men doubted if Aberdeen would even finish the match.

But two weeks earlier Aberdeen had played Celtic at Parkhead in the League – and won 2-1. Suddenly their fans had hope that their long wait to win the Cup again would be ended.

So on April 11 Glasgow faced an invasion of thousands of red and white clad Aberdeen fans who turned the 108,000 crowd at Hampden into a gay whirlpool of colour and sound.

The men from Pittodrie had the easier road to the Final. In the first round they had been drawn at home to Clyde and had coasted to an easy 4-0 win with Davie Robb and Joe Harper sharing the goals.

The second round gave them another home tie against Second Division club Clydebank, and what a fright the Dons got before they struggled through to a 2-1 victory with goals by Robb and centre Jim Forrest.

Next came the quarter-final and another Second Division opponent, Falkirk, although this time Aberdeen were drawn away from home.

It was then that the real drama of the Cup started to build up and the opening chapters of a fairytale which was to thrill Scottish fans were written.

Days before they faced Falkirk at Brockville, Aberdeen were hit by a 'flu epidemic and with eight players missing from training the Dons asked the S.F.A. to have the tie postponed . . . but their request was denied

Derek McKay salutes the Hampden crowd after scoring Aberdeen's second goal in the Cup Final against Celtic.

by Jack Adams

Aberdeen left-back George Murray (No. 3) watches as his keeper Bobby Clark punches a cross ball away from Celtic's Willie Wallace (No. 8) and Jimmy Johnstone (No. 7).

the 34th in their history, Celtic didn't have to leave Glasgow, although they didn't get any easy draws.

Goals by Harry Hood and John Hughes beat Dunfermline 2-1 at Parkhead and Hughes scored two more in Celtic's 4-0 win over Dundee Utd. in the second round. Willie Wallace and young Lou Macari scored the others.

The quarter-final draw paired Celtic with their greatest rivals – Rangers . . . and soccer was set for another explosive match.

In an ugly, bad-tempered brawl of a game Celtic won

Aberdeen inside-left Joe Harper (right) shows his delight after Derek McKay had scored goal number two against Celtic. The other players in the background are; left to right: Henning Boel, George Murray, Arthur Graham and Jim Forrest.

and the game went on.

But the 'flu scare lit the fuse for the explosion that blasted Aberdeen to Cup glory.

For the Aberdeen manager had to reshuffle his squad of players, and he brought in 20-year-old Derek McKay at outside-right.

In the previous season, this highland laddie had been freed by Dundee and was on the verge of quitting football

and emigrating to Canada. But along came Aberdeen with the offer of a two-month trial.

McKay started his first Cup game as an unknown . . . and finished up a hero, scoring the goal which beat Falkirk and put the Dons into the Final again with a chance of revenge for their 2-0 defeat by the Parkhead side in the 1967 Final.

On their way to the Final,

Jimmy Johnstone is booked by referee Bobby Davidson after protesting against the ref's decision to disallow a goal after Bobby Lennox had put the ball in the net.

3-1 with goals by Bobby Lennox, Jimmy Johnstone and the bright new star Davie Hay. When the sparks and bitterness of the battle, in which three men were booked and one sent off, died down it was Dundee's turn to face Jock Stein's stunning soccer machine at Hampden in the semi-final.

Dundee fought bravely, but one slip, one moment of lost concentration by 'keeper Alistair Donaldson only ten minutes from the end, allowed Bobby Lennox to score to give the Parkhead side a 2-1 passport to the Final.

So on to the Final . . . and an ending that sent 15,000 singing, dancing fans back to Aberdeen, with the dream of further glory and magic in the European Cup Winners' Cup this season.

After twenty-seven minutes, Aberdeen were awarded a penalty when a McKay cross hit a defender's hand. *Joe Harper clamly slips the ball past Celtic 'keeper Evan Williams from the penalty spot for Aberdeen's first goal in their 3 – 1 win.*

As the fans argued, as Celtic protested and referee Bobby Davidson booked Tommy Gemmell, one man remained cool in that white-hot furnace of emotion, Aberdeen's inside-left Joe Harper who calmly placed his penalty kick into the corner of the net to put the Dons one goal ahead.

Suddenly the impossible seemed possible and when Celtic had a Bobby Lennox goal ruled out four minutes later they sagged and seemed to lose the spirit and fire which had carried them to the top in football.

It was time for Aberdeen to make sure, to tighten their grip on the Cup they had waited twenty-three years to win . . . and the magic of that young man Derek McKay shone through brighter than ever in the last desperate ten minutes.

With seven minutes to go Derek was the dandiest Don of them all when he smashed the ball high into the net after a great run by Jim Forrest.

Only two minutes remained when Celtic made their last valiant charge and the songs and joy of the Aberdeen fans froze as Bobby Lennox scored for the Celts.

The big question was could Aberdeen hold out, could they stand up to the final all-out blitz we expected from Celtic. Aberdeen had their own answer . . . and again it was that man McKay who raced up the field to score a magnificent goal to make Aberdeen 3-1 winners.

What a victory, what a magic three matches for that man McKay and the other great heroes who ended Aberdeen's 23 year wait.

Aberdeen goal heroes Derek McKay (left) and Joe Harper with the Scottish Cup.

THE YEAR OF THE BABES

It's not so long ago that Rangers star babe Graham Fyfe was playing soccer in the street. Now he passes on some tips to some of his youthful neighbours in Motherwell.

CALL IT THE YEAR of the babes ... the year when the only real challenge to Scotland's soccer establishment came from a bright-eyed, talented bunch of kids.

In a season which started off with a challenging roar to Celtic's stranglehold on success and ended in a whisper as the other clubs fought it out to see who was going to be second once again in the league, it was the babes who made the headlines.

Aberdeen won the Cup, and a million friends, with 21-year-old Martin Buchan as their skipper ... the young-est ever in the Cup Final. And proudly helping him carry the banner of youth were 17-year-old left-winger Arthur Graham and 20-year-old right-winger Derek McKay.

And Celtic kept up their reputation as pacemakers by unleashing a steady stream of new stars into the big team. Davie Hay played his way into the European head-lines and the international squad and George Connelly was another who kept the Parkhead fans singing their victory songs. There was always a talented youngster waiting to step into the first team, ready to make his chal-lenge to stay in the first team. Lou Macari, Vic Davidson, Kenny Dalgleish all got their chance to show the first team players that they were ready, willing and able to slot into the Stein machine.

Rangers too showed that they were willing to give youth its fling and this gave a glimmer of hope to their suc-cess-starved fans who had to endure another season as second bests. When Willie Waddell replaced Davie White as Ibrox team boss after Rangers lost to Gornik in the European Cup Win-ners' Cup, it was the signal for a new deal for the Ibrox babes. Waddell and his as-sistant Willie Thornton were both first team players for Rangers while still teen-agers, so they didn't hesitate to bring in new faces. Iain MacDonald, Graham Fyfe, Alfie Conn and Willie Whyte

by Jack Adams

Keith MacRae . . . 20-year-old Motherwell 'keeper, who made his breakthrough last year as one of Scotland's most talented youngsters. He made his 'cap' debut in the Scottish League v. English League match at Coventry last season.

all got their big breakthrough chance.

Six months after turning senior, Dave McNicol was made captain of Dunfermline as the Fife team climbed aboard the babes bandwagon.

At Tannadice, Dundee United gave Jim Hendry his chance and he quickly showed that he could be one of the most talented midfield players in the country.

The flood of new, exciting talent was amazing and Scotland's soccer future looks bright.

Unfortunately the challenge by the more established stars couldn't shake Celtic from the top . . . although at the start of the season it looked so different, for after the first handful of games Celtic were 9th in the table with Morton, Motherwell, Rangers and Dunfermline leading the way.

Hibs took up the challenge and it looked as if Edinburgh's years as a soccer wilderness would end . . . but the lure of big money

transfers was too much and Hibs sold their two star forwards, Peter Marinello to Arsenal for £100,000 and Peter Cormack to Nottingham Forest for £80,000, and then dropped out of the race as serious challengers.

So once again it was the "Old Firm" battling it out. Celtic really turned on the pressure and moved to the top of the table with a shattering 7-2 win over Dundee United at Parkhead on a cold December night. They were to stay there until the league title was clinched for the fifth successive year with a 0-0 draw at Tynecastle against Hearts on the 28th of March.

And it was left to Celtic to grab the glory in Europe too. At the start of the season we had five clubs in the three European Tourneys. Celtic in the European Cup, Rangers in the Cup Winners' and Kilmarnock, Dundee United and Dunfermline in the Fairs Cup.

Dundee United were the first to go, beaten at home

Alfie Conn . . . one of Ibrox's top discoveries. He made his debut two seasons ago and is at home at right-half or inside-forward.

and away by Newcastle. Dunfermline had a stormy trip beating Bordeaux in the first leg, and the Polish team

Gwardia in the second round before losing to Anderlecht in the quarter-finals. Kilmarnock scraped through against Zurich and the Bulgarian team C.S.K. Slavia but were knocked out by Dinamo Bacau of Rumania.

In the Cup Winners' Cup, Rangers beat the Rumanian

Iain MacDonald . . . made a dream debut for Rangers last season at outside-left against Ayr United when he scored a goal and laid on two in the Ibrox Club's 3 – 0 win.

side Steaua but lost to Gornik of Poland . . . and then fired their manager Davie White 12 hours later.

But the saddest story of the season was the relegation of Partick Thistle for the first time in their history. They went down into the Second Division with Raith Rovers while Falkirk and Cowdenbeath won promotion.

And the little Fife club certainly deserved their champagne celebration for they had previously won promotion way back in 1939 but because of the outbreak of war the leagues were reorganised and Cowdenbeath didn't get into the top league.

Still, that champagne must have tasted well after being on ice for 31 years.

Little Glory...But Lots Of Hope!

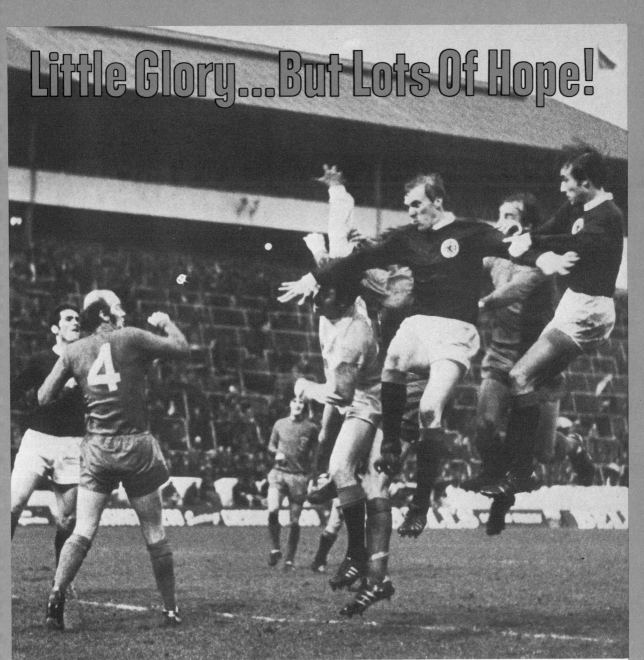

Forward to the rescue! Centre-forward Colin Stein is back to help centre-half Ronnie McKinnon and goalkeeper Jim Cruickshank as the Scots clear this Welsh corner-kick.

AFTER THE BITTER disappointment of not qualifying for the World Cup finals in Mexico, Scotland looked to the home internationals to help restore our tattered international image.

But right from the start these championships became a ghost tournament as each of the four home countries lost star after star because of club commitments.

In this soccer shambles Scotland team boss Bobby Brown decided to experiment, to bring in new faces to fill the gaps left by absent stars.

Our first game was against Ireland at Windsor Park, Belfast. For years this had been a hoodoo ground for Scottish teams.

Bobby Brown took his first gamble by playing youngsters such as Davie Hay, Billy Dickson, Willie Carr and John O'Hare ... and Scotland won 1-0 on a pitch which was a player's nightmare. It was a special nightmare for Ireland's George Best who was sent off for throwing mud at the referee.

The Brown Babes had proved themselves, had shown that they were ready for the big time. John O'Hare, a big, brave striker from Derby County scored the goal, and when Colin Stein of Rangers joined him in the middle in

by Jack Adams

A near miss by Scotland's Alan Gilzean as he slides in to try to intercept a cross from the left. The Irish defence look on anxiously.

Scotland's 'keeper Jim Cruickshank punches clear from Martin Peters as Ronnie McKinnon looks on (left) and Tommy Gemmell covers the goal-line.

the second-half, a great new soccer double-act was born.

The strength and courage of these two were to remain the brightest thing about the week long championships.

Meanwhile England's World Cup squad were held to a draw by Wales and only a spectacular goal by Francis Lee of Manchester City saved them.

On the next Wednesday it was Scotland's turn to face Wales at Hampden. For 90 minutes Scotland gave the Welsh the hiding of their lives, but, as so often happens, they just couldn't get the ball in the net past Wales' Fourth Division 'keeper Tony Millington.

But again we had new stars to praise. Coventry's

West German referee Gerhard Schulenberg called it a 'dive' . . . One hundred and thirty-odd thousand Scottish fans called it several other things – all of them claiming an obvious penalty and indicating England centre-half Brian Labone for a blatant foul that sent Scottish striker Colin Stein flying through the air.

Willie Carr was proving a real find as a midfield player while Davie Hay again proved that he could play any position and do a great job for his team.

In defence too, the Scots had found a new hero in Newcastle's Bobby Moncur. His tremendous tackling and reading of the game had given our rearguard a solid look that had been missing for years.

If there had been little glory then there was certainly a lot of hope for Scotland's soccer future.

After the Wales game it was announced that Bobby Brown had signed a four-year contract as Scottish team boss. Now we had a team and a boss, and together they got to work for the last game of the series, the big one, the game every Scot most wants to win . . . against England.

As 135,000 fans crammed their way into Hampden on a bright April afternoon they knew they would not see England at their brightest.

Their World Cup attack had lost a lot of its sting when Francis Lee wasn't included in the party, it had lost even more when the great Bobby Charlton had to withdraw after breaking a bone in his hand in a training game at Kilmarnock on the eve of the game.

Still there was a lot of strength, a lot of skill, and a lot of danger in the English team which lined up.

To face this final challenge Bobby Brown gave his youngsters another vote of confidence. And to show that Scotland were going out to play football and entertain he brought in little Jimmy Johnstone of Celtic at outside-right.

If the English thought they knew something about football, then they soon found out that they had a lot more to learn . . . mainly from the magical mystery tours of Johnstone who seemed to hypnotise all the English defenders.

From the very start Scotland took over in midfield, where Hay, Carr and John Greig made life hell for the English.

Soon the English tackling became desperate and the German referee, Gerhard Schulenberg, saved England by refusing an obvious penalty when Brian Labone pulled down Colin Stein as the Ranger was racing through. The referee again refused a good penalty claim when Bobby Moore handled a Tommy Gemmell shot.

But it looked as if the Scots must win, despite the referee . . . only again we couldn't squeeze the ball into the net. Things' became even tougher for the Scottish attack when England pulled off their best forward, Peter Thompson, and replaced him with another tough defender in Allan Mullery.

So despite all their pressure, all their good open football, Scotland again failed to score . . . but they certainly handed Sir Alf Ramsey a giant-sized headache to take to Mexico.

Scotland had come through the series unbeaten with a team who played for each other, with bright new stars to give us hope for the future, with the promise that our days in the World Cup wilderness could soon be over.

The England defence crowd out John O'Hare as this Jimmy Johnstone cross beats everybody.

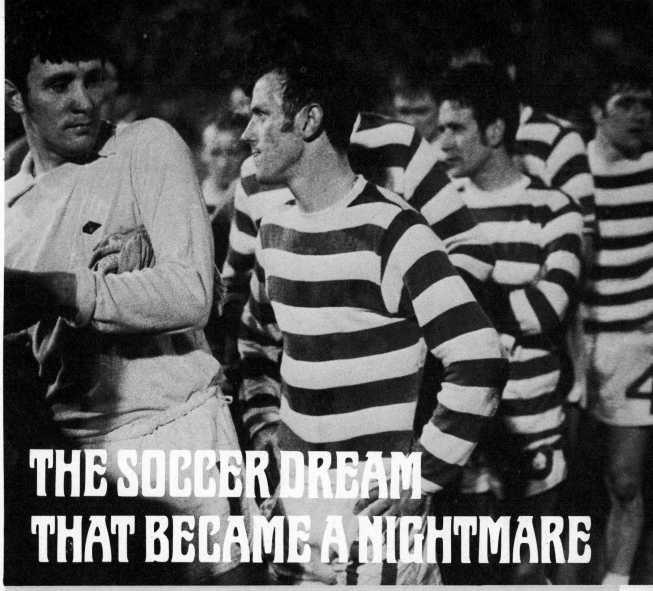

THE SOCCER DREAM THAT BECAME A NIGHTMARE

ITALY HAD never seen anything like it before. It was May and there was a special kind of madness in the air as the soccer spotlight turned its full glare on the city of Milan.

It was European Cup Final time and Celtic, the champions of Scotland, were playing Feyenoord, the champions of Holland, at the San Siro Stadium.

For days the Northern Italian city had been under seige as thousands of fans from Scotland and Holland invaded it by road, rail and air. The streets were a mad, gay riot of colour and noise as the Celtic fans in their green and white mixed with

The tragedy of losing the European Cup is clearly mirrored in these Celtic players' faces as they line up to collect their runners-up medals, Assistant-Manager Sean Fallon (extreme left) watches as Evan Williams, Bobby Lennox, Willie Wallace, Bobby Murdoch and Jim Brogan wait for the presentation.

the Dutch supporters sporting the red and white of their club.

The big game was on May 6, the end of another season . . . the soccer showpiece of Europe.

Celtic had to win. They were the favourites. Their flamboyant attacking style had made them the most feared team in Europe. The Parkhead team were going to blitz their way to their second European Cup win.

This was the soccer dream of every Scot . . . but it was a dream that was to become a living nightmare.

For someone had forgotten to tell Feyenoord that Celtic were invincible.

When the Scots went ahead after 20 minutes with a great shct from Tommy Gemmell, we thought this would be the start of the explosion which would blast Feyenoord, but the explosion fizzled out like a damp squib.

by Jack Adams

Feyenoord 'keeper Eddie Pieters-Graffland is left stranded as Tommy Gemmell (out of picture) crashes home Celtic's goal with a thundering 30-yarder. Team-mate Bobby Murdoch salutes the goal.

Two minutes later the cool, calm Dutch collected the equaliser when their captain Rinus Israel headed past Evan Williams.

From that moment on Feyenoord were the masters of Milan as they strutted and strolled their way about the San Siro pitch. Luckily Celtic held out for 90 minutes and the game went into extra time.

With only 4 minutes of the extra 30 minutes left Feyenoord scored the goal they deserved . . . and rightly the scorer was their Swedish centre Ove Kindvall. Kindvall had been one of the big heroes in a team of heroes.

So a dream died, sadly and without too much of a struggle. Perhaps Celtic manager Jock Stein summed it up best of all when he said:

"It is as simple as this. We beat ourselves. We went out on that field expecting things to happen. The Dutch went out and made things happen."

Celtic are just seconds away from defeat. Evan Williams desperately rushes out to try to block Ove Kindvall's shot . . . but too late. Celtic skipper Billy McNeill, who in desperation had handled the ball only to see it land at Kindvall's feet, looks on in dismay.

The long road to Milan started at the St. Jakob stadium in Basle on the 17th of September, 1969.

Celtic had been drawn against the amateur Swiss club Basle in the first round of the European Cup. In Switzerland they held out for a 0-0 draw and then on the 1st October they won the return leg 2-0.

52,000 singing fans saw Celtic grab a goal in the first minute when Harry Hood scored and then in 65 minutes Tommy Gemmell scored and Celtic were into the second round.

Now things were getting tougher and Celtic were drawn against Benfica. The first leg was played at Parkhead on November 12th and Celtic kept their own private firework display for that night. Benfica, the team with so much talent and so much magic, were completely shattered by the Celtic whirl-wind in front of 80,000 fans. Again Celtic struck quickly and after only 2 minutes little Bertie Auld pushed a free kick back to Tom Gemmell and the left-back flashed a 30-yard shot past the red-shirted Benfica defence. From then on it was torment all the way for Benfica. Willie Wallace scored a great goal just before half-time, then in 69 minutes Harry Hood headed in number 3 from a Murdoch cross.

Celtic were cheered off the field after one of the most devastating performances and they looked certainties for the quarter-final . . . but at that time we had no idea of the drama that was still to come.

For the second leg, on the 26th November, Celtic re-turned in triumph to Lisbon where they had won the Euro-pean Cup in 1967. Maybe it was just too much of a gala

occasion, maybe for once the so professional Celts under-estimated their oppo-nents. For what had looked such an easy job almost be-came a tragedy for Celtic and a disaster for Scottish foot-ball. This was a different Benfica from the team Celtic had slaughtered only a fort-night previously.

Eusebio scored with a brilliant header in 36 minutes and before Celtic could really recover Graca raced through to score a second two minutes later.

In the second-half Celtic fought desperately to control the game as Benfica went all out for the goal that would give them another chance in

extra time. The tension was unbearable, the noise deaf-ening in Lisbon's famous stadium of Light . . . and then the unbelievable happened and Benfica equalised.

In the last second of injury time Celtic gave away a free kick, and as they lined up their defensive wall Diamantino slammed the ball through a gap and into the net with the last kick of the game.

Now it was all pandemo-nium. The fans didn't know whether the goal would count or whether it had been scored too late. It wasn't until the shattered teams lined up to face 30 gruelling minutes of extra time that they realised

We're through! Bertie Auld, ball in one hand, a Leeds jersey in the other and a hat on his head, shows his joy after the Parkhead club's European Cup semi-final success over Leeds.

the goal had stood.

If what happened in those first 90 minutes was torrid then the real tightrope tension was still to come.

Somehow Celtic pulled themselves back up off the floor on the invisible strings of courage and held out for the longest 30 minutes of their lives.

The game ended with the teams still locked in a 3-3 aggregate and now came the moment of truth as the Dutch referee Van Raavens called the two captains Billy McNeill of Celtic and Mario Coluna to his room to settle the epic tie.

And as the silent drama was played out deep in the heart of the giant stadium, 80,000 Portuguese fans waited on the terracings for the results.

Inside the referee's room a silver Dutch Guilder was spun into the air by Celtic captain Billy McNeill . . . it came down heads and Celtic

were through to the quarter-finals.

And so on to the quarter-finals and the first leg home draw against Fiorentina at Parkhead on the 4th of March.

Bertie Auld was the hero of this game with a brilliant performance which was praised by both his own boss Jock Stein and Fiorentina boss Bruno Pesaloa.

Celtic again played brilliantly and Auld had a hand in their 3 goals scoring a beauty himself and making the others.

The inside-left shot his team ahead after 31 minutes and 4 minutes after the interval Celtic struck again. Auld sent over a dangerous cross and Carpenetti, in trying to clear, deflected the ball past his own 'keeper.

One minute from time Wallace made it 3-0 when he headed home after Hood had nodded on an Auld cross.

A fortnight later Celtic went to Florence for the

return game . . . this time there was to be no repeat of that Lisbon nightmare. Despite losing 1-0, Celtic became the first British club to knock an Italian team out of the European Cup over two legs.

But although marching into the semi-final on a 3-1 aggregate an angry Jock Stein hit out after the game at the referee. Stein said, "I have never known worse refereeing in all the games I have seen in Europe. Everything was for the Italians. In these circumstances I rate this our finest performance in Europe."

Although losing a 36 minute goal to Chiarugi, Celtic gave a great display of defensive football and wee Jimmy Johnstone became the new hero of the Italian fans with a magnificent performance of ball control and courage.

The semi-final draw threw up the game that all Britain had been waiting for . . . Leeds v. Celtic. The English

Leeds left-back Terry Cooper and 'keeper Gary Sprake stand frozen in dismay . . . Billy Bremner looks on from a distance . . . Jack Charlton pitches to the ground beside man-of-the-moment John Hughes who watches his header cross the line for Celtic's first goal.